Learn to Read

Level 8 Workbook

Early Fluent Readers

Second Grade
Ages 7–8

This workbook includes these foundational reading skills:

- decoding words with long- and short-vowel teams and dipthongs (*-oy, -oi, -ou, -ow*)
- decoding words with triple-beginning blends and silent-letter combinations
- decoding two-syllable words by breaking the word into syllables
- recognizing commonly used sight words
- reading stories with purpose and understanding

Credits

Design Team
Russell Ginns
Amy Kraft
TJ Trochlil McGreevy
Christopher Medellin
Dorothy M. Taguchi, Ph.D.

Senior Producer
Amy Kraft

Senior Director of Product Development
Russell Ginns

Editorial Direction
The Linguistic Edge

Educational Advisors
Sheila Mandel, Ed.M.
Sonja Roseman, Ed.M.
Dorothy M. Taguchi, Ph.D.

Story Writer
Michael Artin

Story Illustrations
Kelly Kennedy (pages 8–9, 26–27)
Joshua Nash (pages 4–5, 12–13, 40–41)
Bob Ostrom (pages 22–23, 48–49)
Tamara Petrosino (pages 30–31, 44–45)

Alphabet Illustrations
Bryan Langdo

Design and Layout
Two Red Shoes Design

Special Thanks
Leslie Alacbay, Amy Bevilacqua, Kelly Dickens, Adina Ficano, Judy Harris, and Robert Pugh

© 2020 Sandviks, HOP, Inc. All Rights Reserved.
No part of this publication may be reproduced, stored in any retrieval system or transmitted, in any form or by any means, electronic, mechanical or otherwise, without prior written permission of the publisher.
Printed in China.

Contents

Lesson Overview iv
Level 7 Review vi

Unit 1 1
   Lesson 1: oy, oi 2
   Lesson 2: ou, ow 6
   Lesson 3: au, aw 10
   Lesson 4: all, sight words *where, nice,*
     don't, been, give, many 14
   Review 18

Unit 2 19
   Lesson 5: oo 20
   Lesson 6: igh, ind 24
   Lesson 7: shr, str 28
   Lesson 8: scr, spr, sight words *away,*
     their, walk, once, always, seven 32
   Review 36

Unit 3 37
   Lesson 9: spl, squ 38
   Lesson 10: kn, wr 42
   Lesson 11: Soft c, Soft g 46
   Lesson 12: Two-Syllable Words,
     sight words *before, after, never, again,*
     work, because 50
   Review 54

Lesson Overview

Every lesson follows the same approach: **Learn, Practice, Read.**

Select "Start Here" on the DVD or online* for an overview of how to use the program. Guidance in this workbook will walk you through every step in the process.

Learn
Learn to read new words by watching the lesson on the DVD or online and then reading the new words in the workbook.

Practice
Then practice reading the new sound combinations and words in the workbook.

Read
Now you're ready to read. Each lesson ends with a story in the workbook or a storybook. Every story and book is composed of words that your child has learned to read so far in the program.

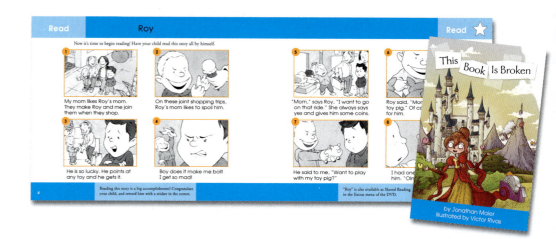

*Visit **my.hookedonphonics.com** to set up your online account.

Celebrate

As you know, reading is a big deal. Each time your child reads a story or book, celebrate by placing a sticker in the workbook. This also provides a helpful marker to remember where to begin next time.

Tips for Success
- **Set a good pace.** Work at a pace that's right for your child, whether it's once a week or four times a week.
- **Don't overdo it.** Fit the lessons into your child's attention span, generally between 20 and 30 minutes.
- **Repetition and review are important.** Don't hesitate to review previous lessons before moving on.
- **Talk about the books and stories.** Engaging your child in a conversation about what he's reading helps stimulate his thinking and comprehension.
- **Read to your child every day.** The more you share the love of reading with your child, the more your child will want to read.

Throughout this workbook, you'll see parent tips in the blue bar along the bottom of the page. These tips are designed to help you answer questions your child might have about things that are new to him. They'll also give you ideas on how to extend the learning at home and on the go.

New lessons build on previous ones, so make sure your child has mastered the current lesson before moving forward.

Level 7 Review

Use this page to determine if your child is ready to start **Learn to Read** Level 8, which builds on the lessons of Level 7. Starting at each number, have your child read the words going across from left to right. If she can do this easily, she's ready to begin.

1. cheek fry wait goal quite rear shape target

2. share barn dream day life theme girl core

3. forget sport burn made tune slow penny verse

Unit 1 — Introduction

To begin this unit, watch the Unit 1 introduction on the DVD or online. This will walk you and your child through the sounds and words that he will be learning in this unit.

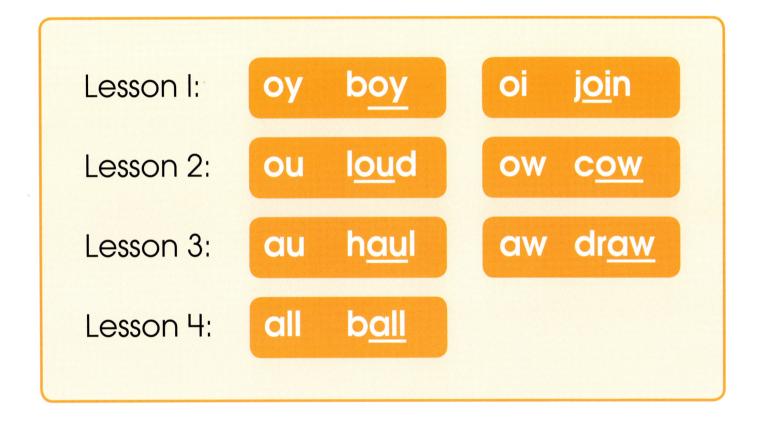

Lesson 1: oy boy   oi join
Lesson 2: ou loud   ow cow
Lesson 3: au haul   aw draw
Lesson 4: all ball

Watching the Unit 1 introduction may be all you want to do on the first day. Judge your child's attention span to see if he's ready to start the first lesson immediately or if you should wait until another day.

Lesson 1: oy, oi

Learn

Start by watching Lesson 1 on the DVD or online, then return to this page. Have your child use his finger as a guide working from left to right, stopping at each word while he says the word out loud. Have him repeat this a few times until he's ready to move on.

oy boy

→ boy   joy   toy   coy   soy   Roy

oi join

→ join   oil   void   boil   coin   soil
→ oink   broil   joint   spoil   moist   point

If your child hesitates on a word, gently say the word out loud, and have him repeat after you. He's ready to begin practicing when he can read this page with little hesitation.

Practice

Starting at each number, have your child read the words going across from left to right.

1. soy · toy · boy · Roy · coy · joy · toy · soy

2. moist · boil · join · oink · oil · joint · void · broil

3. point · coy · soil · boy · coin · Roy · joy · spoil

Read
Roy

Now it's time to begin reading! Have your child read this story all by himself.

My mom likes Roy's mom. They make Roy and me join them when they shop.

On these joint shopping trips, Roy's mom likes to spoil him.

He is so lucky. He points at any toy and he gets it.

Boy does it make me boil! I get so mad!

Reading this story is a big accomplishment! Congratulate your child, and reward him with a sticker in the corner.

Read

"Mom," says Roy, "I want to go on that ride." She always says yes and gives him some coins.

Roy said, "Mom, I want that toy pig." Of course she got it for him.

He said to me, "Want to play with my toy pig?"

I had one thing to say to him. "Oink!"

"Roy" is also available as a Shared Reading on the Main Menu of the DVD and online.

Learn | **Lesson 2: ou, ow**

Watch Lesson 2 on the DVD or online. Then return here. Have your child use her finger as a guide, stopping at each word while she says the word out loud. Have her repeat this a few times until she's ready to move on.

ou loud

→ loud   out   cloud   mouse   ouch   found
→ crouch shout   mouth   count   house   ground

ow cow

→ cow   bow   now   crowd   down   brow
→ plow   crown   fowl   town   how   brown
→ drown   owl   growl   clown   frown   howl

Practice

Starting at each number, have your child read the words going across from left to right.

1) found | house | out | mouth | ouch | ground | shout | cloud

2) brown | now | crown | owl | how | clown | town | crowd

3) brow | count | cow | growl | mouse | frown | loud | down

Read — The Showdown

1
The house is quiet. There is nothing even as loud as a mouse.

2
My toy cow is missing. I frown. There's a cow robber in town.

3
I scout around. I will find the cow robber.

4
Now I hear a sound—the sound of a hound.

Read

5. I crouch down. Shep is under the couch with my cow in his mouth.

6. "I found you, cow robber!" I shout. Shep comes out and growls.

7. This is a showdown!

8. The hound is no match for me. The cow is mine!

Learn | **Lesson 3: au, aw**

Watch Lesson 3 on the DVD or online. Then return here. Have your child use his finger as a guide, stopping at each word while he says the word out loud. Have him repeat this a few times until he's ready to move on.

au   haul

→   haul   Paul   launch   haunt   fault   gauze

aw   draw

→   draw   saw   law   jaw   claw   thaw
→   yawn   flaw   crawl   dawn   hawk   lawn

Practice

Starting at each number, have your child read the words going across from left to right.

1. haunt Paul fault gauze haul launch haunt fault

2. claw dawn jaw draw hawk saw yawn flaw

3. down crawl law crowd lawn joy thaw found

The Red-Tailed Hawk

The red-tailed hawk is a big bird. It eats meat—mice, rabbits, snakes, and birds. When you see a hawk launch off a perch, look at his tail. If you see red, that is a red-tailed hawk.

When a hawk wants to eat, he sits and waits, looking. He can see much better than we can. From very far, he can see a mouse crawl in the grass. He can see a snake in the lawn.

Read

He launches from his perch—and then look out! He can grab a rabbit in his claws and haul it into the sky. Hawks do not thaw, bake, or fry their meals. They eat them raw! And while hawks do not have jaws with teeth, they can rip their meal up with a sharp beak.

From dawn till dusk, mice and rabbits look to the sky. It is the law of the land: Watch out for the hawk!

As your child reads more and more, encourage him to explore different genres, including both fiction and nonfiction.

Learn

Lesson 4: all

Watch Lesson 4 on the DVD or online. Then return here. Have your child use her finger as a guide, stopping at each word while she says the word out loud. Have her repeat this a few times until she's ready to move on.

Helper Words

Learn

"Helper words" are commonly used words that either can't be sounded out or have sounds your child is not yet ready to learn. Also referred to as *sight words*, these words are learned through repetition. You've already seen them in the Lesson 4 video. Now repeat them with your child. Have her point to and read each word five times, or until she reads them easily.

To make learning helper words more like a game, call out a color and have her read the word on that color.

Practice

Starting at each number, have your child read the words going across from left to right.

1 | tall | hall | small | wall | call | stall | all | fall

2 | been | mall | nice | don't | ball | many | where | give

3 | jaw | fault | down | coin | call | mouse | crawl | nice

This Book Is Broken

Read

Your child is ready for the book *This Book Is Broken*. Before reading, have her look at the cover and read the title. Ask her what she thinks the book might be about. After reading, use these questions to discuss the book.

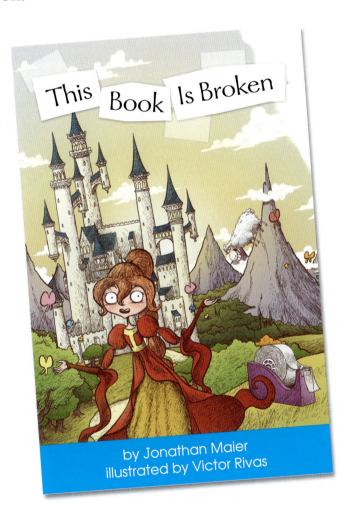

Discussion Questions

- How did the book break?
- What are some of the things that are wrong with the book?
- Who is trying to fix the book? How?
- Why does Ted show up on the wrong page?
- What happened to the princess's crown?
- Try going back to each page and imagine what it would be like if the page were fixed. What would be different about each page?

Visit **my.hookedonphonics.com** for additional activities after each lesson.

Unit I Review

Have your child place her finger on the arrow. As she follows the path with her finger, have her read each word she encounters until she reaches the star.

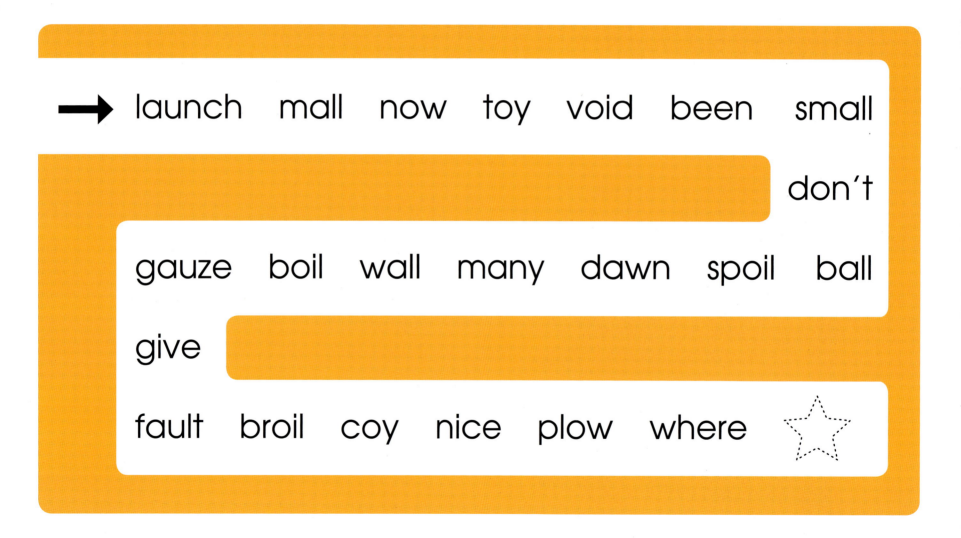

As your child reads these words, note any trouble spots. If she has difficulty with words with the same sounds, it's a good idea to repeat that lesson before moving forward.

Unit 2 — Introduction

To begin this unit, watch the Unit 2 introduction on the DVD or online. This will walk you and your child through the sounds and words that he will be learning in this unit.

Lesson 5:	oo m<u>oo</u>n	oo b<u>oo</u>k
Lesson 6:	igh ni<u>gh</u>t	ind f<u>ind</u>
Lesson 7:	shr <u>shr</u>imp	str <u>str</u>aw
Lesson 8:	scr <u>scr</u>atch	spr <u>spr</u>ing

Before beginning Unit 2, you may want to re-watch the Unit 1 introduction as a review.

Learn

Lesson 5: oo

Watch Lesson 5 on the DVD or online. Then return here. Have your child use his finger as a guide, stopping at each word while he says the word out loud. Have him repeat this a few times until he's ready to move on.

oo m<u>oo</u>n

→ m<u>oo</u>n   z<u>oo</u>   c<u>oo</u>l   r<u>oo</u>m   f<u>oo</u>d   l<u>oo</u>p

→ b<u>oo</u>t   t<u>oo</u>th   g<u>oo</u>se   sc<u>oo</u>p   br<u>oo</u>m   sp<u>oo</u>n

oo b<u>oo</u>k

→ b<u>oo</u>k   w<u>oo</u>l   l<u>oo</u>k   g<u>oo</u>d   h<u>oo</u>f   f<u>oo</u>t

→ t<u>oo</u>k   h<u>oo</u>d   w<u>oo</u>d   sh<u>oo</u>k   cr<u>oo</u>k   st<u>oo</u>d

There are two parts in this lesson because *oo* makes two different sounds. Say *moon* and then *book*, and notice how they sound different.

Practice

Starting at each number, have your child read the words going across from left to right.

1 loop tooth zoo spoon room moon scoop cool

2 foot wood shook book good crook look hood

3 goose took food boot stood broom wool hoof

Read
Cowboy Paul's High-Noon Lunch

Kids' Meals

Rope the Steer: A pile of meatballs and noodle loops as big as grandma's hoop skirt! You need a fork and a spoon for this one.

Boot on the Hoof: A foot-long hot dog is what I mean! Just like one cooked on a wood fire.

Took from the Brook: Fish sticks, by the look of it. Fresh off the hook and on your plate.

Read

And leave room for . . .

Cool Hand Scoop: Dig your spoon into two big scoops of ice cream.

Howl at the Moon: A black and white cookie.

I could sink my tooth into that!

When you are in a restaurant, use your waiting time to see how much of the menu your child can read.

Lesson 6: igh, ind

Learn

Watch Lesson 6 on the DVD or online. Then return here. Have your child use her finger as a guide, stopping at each word while she says the word out loud. Have her repeat this a few times until she's ready to move on.

igh night

→ night   high   right   light   sigh   fight
→ tight   might   fright   bright   thigh   flight

ind find

→ find   mind   kind   wind   grind   blind

Practice

Starting at each number, have your child read the words going across from left to right.

1 | might | sigh | night | flight | right | high | fright | light

2 | kind | find | grind | wind | blind | mind | find | kind

3 | thigh | room | fight | mind | bright | hood | tight | hall

Read

Fright in the Night

Ben woke up one night. Was it just a dream, or did he hear a sound?

By the light of the moon, he caught sight of some kind of beast!

It was winding its way close to him. He was so scared.

And then it went right under his bed!

Congratulations! This is the halfway point of this workbook. Be sure and tell your child how well she's doing!

Read

5

He shook with fright. His chest felt tight. He might have to fight this thing!

6

In the dark he was blind. He took his flashlight and bent down.

7

What would he find? Wait . . . wait . . . then he turned on the bright light!

8

Ben sat back with a sigh. It was just his cat!

"Fright in the Night" is also available as a Shared Reading on the Main Menu of the DVD and online.

Learn

Lesson 7: shr, str

Watch Lesson 7 on the DVD or online. Then return here. Have your child use his finger as a guide, stopping at each word while he says the word out loud. Have him repeat this a few times until he's ready to move on.

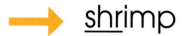

→ shrimp   shred   shrink   shrub   shrug   shrank

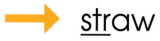

→ straw   strap   street   string   strike   strong
→ streak   strand   strict   strain   stripe   stress

Practice

Starting at each number, have your child read the words going across from left to right.

1 | shrug | shrink | shred | shrimp | shrank | shrub | shrink | shrug

2 | strike | streak | strap | strain | stress | street | strict | string

3 | wood | straw | right | stripe | strand | blind | strong | yawn

The Dress

My mom gave me a nice new dress
But then said, with a wink,
"Don't get it wet, I have to stress.
Take care, for it might shrink."

I gave my mom a little shrug
and said, "Oh Mom! Don't whine.
My last dress shrank, but with a tug
or two it fit me fine!"

So I went out, and on the street
A rain started to fall.
A little stream ran by my feet.
I did not care at all.

But then it struck! A streak of pain!
It had me in its grip.
The dress had shrunk. I pulled.
   I strained.
I think I felt it rip.

Then the rain fell harder. It
Was a stroke of bad luck.
A strand of hair would not have fit
in without getting stuck.

I could not move or shift a strap,
so I just stood there limp,
And thought, "Well this is quite a trap,
A dress made for a shrimp!"

Rhyming stories and books are great for phonics practice. Have your child read and identify the rhymes. Ask him to name additional rhymes.

Learn

Lesson 8: scr, spr

Watch Lesson 8 on the DVD or online. Then return here. Have your child use her finger as a guide, stopping at each word while she says the word out loud. Have her repeat this a few times until she's ready to move on.

scr scratch

→ scratch   scram   scrap   scrub   scrape   scream

→ screen   scrimp   scrawl   screech   script   scribe

spr spring

→ spring   sprawl   sprint   sprain   sprung   spray

→ sprang   sprout   sprite   spree   spry

Helper Words

Learn

Have your child point to and read each word. Then call out a color and have her read the word written on that color.

As your child learns the word *seven*, she can now read the numbers one through ten. Write them on a piece of paper, mixing the order. Have her read each number and write down the numeral next to each word.

Practice

Starting at each number, have your child read the words going across from left to right.

1 scram | scrape | scrawl | scrub | scratch | script | screen | scream

2 spray | sprite | sprawl | sprang | spry | spring | spree | sprain

3 always | their | scrap | once | sprint | away | seven | walk

The Puppy Look

Read

Your child is ready for her next book, *The Puppy Look*. Before reading, have her look at the cover and read the title. Ask her what she thinks the book might be about. After reading, use these questions to discuss the book.

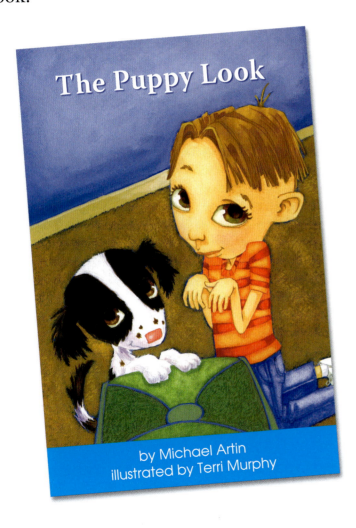

Discussion Questions
- What does Sprite get Mom and Dad to do by giving them the puppy look?
- Why does Bucky pretend he's a dog?
- What does Bucky like and not like about being a dog?
- Does the puppy look work when Bucky tries it? How?
- Why does Bucky stop pretending he's a dog?
- What kind of animal would you pretend to be? Why?

As your child reads longer books, don't pressure her to read the whole book in one sitting. If it's too much for her, try coming back to it another day.

Review

Unit 2 Review

Have your child place her finger on the arrow. As she follows the path with her finger, have her read each word she encounters until she reaches the star.

→ screech   tight   spree   boot   always   streak

tooth

seven   spring   right   shred   once   walk   stripe

their

strap   wind   away   shrink   crook   strict   ☆

Remember, for more activities, visit **my.hookedonphonics.com**.

Unit 3

Introduction

To begin this unit, watch the Unit 3 introduction on the DVD or online. This will walk you and your child through the sounds and words that he will be learning in this unit.

Lesson 9:	spl s**pl**ash	squ **squ**are
Lesson 10:	kn **kn**ife	wr **wr**ite
Lesson 11:	c mi**c**e	g pa**g**e
Lesson 12:	car toon **cartoon**	

The unit introductions and lessons on the DVD and online provide great review when you're in between lessons.

Lesson 9: spl, squ

Learn

Watch Lesson 9 on the DVD or online. Then return here. Have your child use his finger as a guide, stopping at each word while he says the word out loud. Have him repeat this a few times until he's ready to move on.

→ splash   splat   splint   split   spleen

→ square   squeak   squint   squirt   squawk   squish
→ squirm   squeal   squid   squeeze

Practice

Starting at each number, have your child read the words going across from left to right.

1. splat   splash   split   spleen   splint   splash   splat   split

2. squish   square   squeeze   squirt   squeal   squint   squid   squeak

3. sprint   squirm   scrape   spleen   shrink   squawk   straw   shrank

At the Beach

I love the sounds of the beach, like the squawk of gulls and the crash of waves as they split the air.

Listen! Kids in the waves start to squeak and squeal when they see jellyfish!

You might be scared to step on a crab. The crab is scared you will squish him!

Those men always shout when they catch a fish. Look, one is about to splash out of the water.

Read

5 Watch as I squeeze a squid. It will squirt ink in your face! That will teach you!

6 Look at that. A gull drops a clam on the ground to split it open. Now the gull can eat.

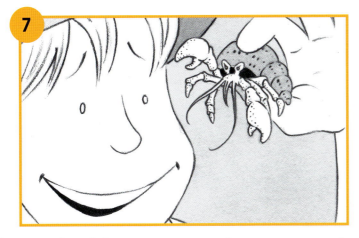

7 See what happens when you pick up that shell? That crab will squirm like mad until you put him down.

8 If you squint, you might see the big splash of a whale far off. Quite a tail, huh?

Learn

Lesson 10: kn, wr

Watch Lesson 10 on the DVD or online. Then return here. Have your child use her finger as a guide, stopping at each word while she says the word out loud. Have her repeat this a few times until she's ready to move on.

kn knife

→ knife   knee   know   knock   kneel   knit

→ knelt   knob   knot   knight   knack   known

wr write

→ write   wrap   wry   wreck   wring   wrist

→ wrong   wrote   wrench   wren   wreath   wrung

In this lesson, *k* and *w* are silent letters. If your child is having trouble, have her first imagine that the silent letter is not there and have her try reading the word again.

Practice

Starting at each number, have your child read the words going across from left to right.

1. knot · known · kneel · know · knife · knack · knee · knight

2. wrist · wreath · wrap · write · wrench · wring · wrote · wry

3. knob · wrong · knelt · wren · knock · wreck · knit · wrung

Read

Miss Knell

Miss Knell likes to knit in class. I wrote Jordan a note about it, but he lost the note.

I knelt down to look for it, but I couldn't find it. Then Miss Knell called out my name.

I stood up so fast that I knocked my head on the desk.

Miss Knell had my note! She said, "Polly, did you write this?"

Read

5 I felt a knot in my gut. "Yes, I wrote the note. I know it was wrong."

6 I was scared she would wring my neck, or maybe slap my wrist. But she smiled.

7 She said, "Did you know a wit has a knack for saying smart and funny things?"

8 Miss Knell is proud of the note. She hung it on the wall. The note says, "Miss Knell is a knit wit."

"Miss Knell" is also available as a Shared Reading on the Main Menu of the DVD and online.

Lesson 11: Soft c, Soft g

Learn

Watch Lesson 11 on the DVD or online. Then return here. Have your child use his finger as a guide, stopping at each word while he says the word out loud. Have him repeat this a few times until he's ready to move on.

c mi<u>c</u>e

→ mi<u>c</u>e   <u>c</u>ent   fa<u>c</u>e   <u>c</u>inch   dan<u>c</u>e   fen<u>c</u>e

→ sin<u>c</u>e   pea<u>c</u>e   twi<u>c</u>e   pla<u>c</u>e   prin<u>c</u>e   for<u>c</u>e

g pa<u>g</u>e

→ pa<u>g</u>e   a<u>g</u>e   <u>g</u>em   ca<u>g</u>e   <u>g</u>el   ra<u>g</u>e

→ <u>g</u>erm   <u>g</u>ene   sta<u>g</u>e   lar<u>g</u>e   hin<u>g</u>e   plun<u>g</u>e

For this lesson, explain to your child that sometimes *c* makes the **s** sound and *g* makes the **j** sound. These are called soft sounds.

Practice

Starting at each number, have your child read the words going across from left to right.

1 dance   peace   place   mice   prince   force   cinch   face

2 germ   stage   plunge   page   gel   large   age   hinge

3 twice   cage   cent   rage   since   gem   fence   gene

Read

Stage Mouse

Read

Comic books and graphic novels can be a great way to get kids, especially reluctant readers, hooked on reading.

Learn

Lesson 12: Two-Syllable Words

Watch Lesson 12 on the DVD or online. Then return here. Have your child use her finger as a guide, stopping at each word while she says the word out loud. Have her repeat this a few times until she's ready to move on.

car toon cartoon

→ car toon cartoon → jig saw jigsaw

→ pen cil pencil → mush room mushroom

→ light ning lightning → see saw seesaw

→ rac coon raccoon → prin cess princess

→ bam boo bamboo → pow der powder

This lesson is designed to show kids that they don't need to be afraid of big words. When your child breaks these words into smaller parts, she'll start seeing words and sounds that look familiar.

Helper Words

Learn

Have your child point to and read each word. Then call out a color and have him read the word written on that color.

before	after	never
again	work	because

Practice

Starting at each number, have your child read the words going across from left to right.

1 | seesaw | bamboo | mushroom | princess | jigsaw | powder | raccoon

2 | never | cartoon | work | because | pencil | before | after

3 | again | dance | kneel | wrong | lightning | squawk | splash

Shoes in the Night

Read

Your child is ready for her next book, *Shoes in the Night*. Before reading, have her look at the cover and read the title. Ask her what she thinks the book might be about. After reading, use these questions to discuss the book.

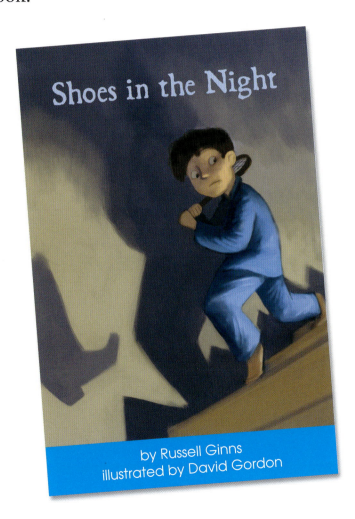

Discussion Questions
- Why does the boy have trouble sleeping?
- What do the shoes do?
- What do you think the boy thinks when he sees the shoe party?
- What happens as the shoes start to trip and bump?
- What does the boy do to help the shoes?
- How does the boy feel differently about the shoes at the end of the book?

As an activity, have your child come up with a new verse for *Shoes in the Night*. What else can shoes do? Can she make her verse rhyme?

Review

Unit 3 Review

Have your child place her finger on the arrow. As she follows the path with her finger, have her read each word she encounters until she reaches the star.

→ cage   split   wrench   never   mushroom   germ

force

before   knot   again   princess   because   squish

work

cartoon   large   prince   after   knife   splat

To reinforce all of the lessons you've now completed, visit **my.hookedonphonics.com**.